GO LOVE YOURSELF

HELP FOR THE JOURNEY TO MENTAL AND EMOTIONAL WELLNESS

ZACHARY LEVI

HARPER
HORIZON

Published by Harper Horizon, an imprint of HarperCollins Focus LLC.

Portions of this book were excerpted and adapted from *Radical Love: Learning to Accept Yourself and Others* (9780785236757).

Any internet addresses, phone numbers, or company or product information printed in this book are offered as a resource and are not intended in any way to be or to imply an endorsement by Harper Horizon, nor does Harper Horizon vouch for the existence, content, or services of these sites, phone numbers, companies, or products beyond the life of this book.

The information in this book has been carefully researched by the author, and is intended to be a source of information only. Readers are urged to consult with their physicians or other professional advisors to address specific medical or other issues. The author and the publisher assume no responsibility for any injuries suffered or damages incurred during or as a result of the use or application of the information contained herein.

ISBN 978-1-4003-4620-2 (Ebook)
ISBN 978-1-4003-4622-6 (Audio)
ISBN 978-1-4003-4621-9 (PB)

Library of Congress Control Number: 2022930124

Printed in the United States of America

24 25 26 27 28 LBC 5 4 3 2 1

Introduction

If you are looking for a book filled with super unrealistic positivity that only exists in a G-rated world, then close this book now and walk away. This book isn't for you. This book is for people who have been to hell and have the grit to keep moving forward despite their past trauma and struggles. I don't sugarcoat anything. I share everything—the good and the bad. This book is for people who know they have hit rock bottom but still want more out of life. If this sounds like you, you are my people.

We are taught not to share our complete selves, so when someone asks us how we are doing we reply with *fine, good,* or even *great.* The honest response should sound a lot more like *hanging in there, okay,* or *not great.* We begin to believe the lies that we tell others. And I'm not talking about believing in the sense that we think we are doing fantastic, but instead we create armor that shields the world from our true feelings. The lies that we live break down our mental wellness. At least, that is what I believe.

While my life on the big screen probably seems glamorous, my life is far from that. I am a product of generational trauma and abuse. As a child I was neglected and never really loved or liked myself. It took me hitting rock bottom to finally get the help I needed so I could heal. I have written this book because I would like to share my healing journey with you. I believe we all have a purpose in life, and I know that we are supposed to learn from one another so we can live out our purpose.

I have also learned that mental wellness is part of living and isn't something that can be fixed by reading this book or just talking to a therapist. Mental wellness is a culmination of resources, and being part of your wellness journey is a privilege that I don't take lightly. I want you to learn from my mistakes and realize that you are not alone. There are so many people in the world battling the same struggles and feeling the same mixed bag of emotions you are experiencing. Even though tracing trauma and processing emotions probably feels overwhelming and scary, the journey of mental wellness is worth it. The first step you must take is learning how to love yourself, and that's what I'm sharing with you—how I learned to love myself.

Each day I encourage you to read one entry and respond to the prompts. You can respond verbally to yourself, write answers in a journal, or take notes on an app. I want to preface this with reiterating this isn't some book proclaiming to fix all your problems, but it is a resource that will help you kick off or continue your mental wellness journey.

DAY 1

Reacting vs. Responding

It had been five years since my TV show *Chuck* had been canceled by NBC. I'd worked steadily since, but my phone wasn't ringing off the hook with major offers. I was secretly afraid that my run as an actor was all but finished. On top of that, while most of my friends were off getting hitched and settling down, my marriage had imploded, just like every other relationship I'd ever had. I was closing in on thirty-seven, alone, with no family. I'd packed my entire life into a U-Haul and moved to Austin from Los Angeles with big dreams that were going to change my life, dreams that had given me a newfound sense of mission and purpose, but now I was beginning to question whether I'd made a terrible mistake.

What I can say, in hindsight, is that I was suffering from a tremendous amount of anxiety at the time. I had, in fact, been wrestling with anxiety and depression and fear and self-loathing my entire life. I just hadn't known it. I 100 percent did not think of myself as someone with serious mental health issues. I didn't know what anxiety and depression really were, at least not from a clinical point of view. When I finally did learn the depths of their meaning, it was a revelation: "Wait a minute . . . if this is what anxiety is, then this is what I've been feeling almost every waking moment for most of my life."

Up until that summer I'd always managed to white-knuckle my way through my problems, self-medicating and finding ways to keep myself propped up, without ever realizing how emotionally fragile I was. And when it came to the subject of my own mental health, I was functionally illiterate.

Coming to terms with the full scope of my ignorance about mental health was upsetting for me. I'm a person who's always prided myself on my ability to tackle complex problems and figure them out. One of my favorite books as a kid was this oversize picture book called *The Way Things Work*. It had page after page of these fun cross-section illustrations showing you "This is how a pulley works" and "This is how an elevator works." I used to sit and look through it for hours. I think I've always had more of an engineer's brain. That brain has helped me many times in my career—having the ability to analyze how the business of Hollywood operates, taking the system apart to figure out the best way to navigate it. But that same mind was completely flummoxed when it came to understanding how its own inner mechanisms functioned. I didn't understand the cause and effect between the traumas I'd experienced as a child and the behaviors I was wrestling with as an adult. I didn't understand that so much of my insecurity came from outsourcing my sense of self-worth to forces beyond my control. I didn't understand that the reason my marriage had ended wasn't because I'd failed but because I was broken.

We don't respond to our negative feelings; we react to them. To respond is to carefully weigh the causes and consequences of a decision while understanding our own motivations for making that decision. How can you make an effort to respond to your negative feelings instead of just react?

DAY 2

Mental Well-Being

Taking care of your mind should be no more embarrassing than taking care of your teeth. We all need to be proactive—to brush and floss our minds to root out the lies we tell ourselves and the bad programming that drives so much of our behavior. We don't. We do the opposite. We pretend and project out to the world that "I'm great!" and "We're great!" and "Everything's fine!" But it's not always fine, and because we refuse to admit that, we do nothing, and all of a sudden what started out as a little cavity is now in need of a root canal.

Society places a terrible stigma on mental illness. We judge people for it in ways that we never would for other kinds of health issues. If you tell someone you're physically ill, they say, "Oh gosh. I'm so sorry. What's the matter? Talk to me." There's no stigma attached to it. From cancer to the common cold, people want to make sure you're okay. But when you swap out "physical illness" with "mental illness," then people seem to start pondering, *Well, how unstable is this person? Is it time for a straitjacket and a rubber room?* Which makes us ashamed to talk about it. We shouldn't be, but we are—and I was, like so many other people.

Trauma bends our minds into incorrect thinking patterns, so much so that we can barely see or think our way around them. It took me a long time to recognize how much help and healing I needed.

What trauma has caused you to adopt a negative thinking pattern? When did you recognize it? What proactive steps do you take to stay mentally healthy?

DAY 3

Get Help

If you're feeling overwhelmed, run-down, fearful, stressed out, anxious, depressed, alone, or anything that may be robbing you of your peace or your joy, talk to someone. Do *not* believe the lie that you are going through this alone. Because you aren't. You could be sitting next to someone, right this second, who struggles with the same issues that you do. Maybe that person can help you. We are all in this together.

From the minute we come into this world, even though we're not aware of it, we're trying to feel that we belong, that we matter. We look to our parents and our friends and our family and our school and our society, and we ask them, "Who am I? Do I have worth in this world? Do I have purpose in this life?"

The answer, without question, is *"Yes. You do."* Unfortunately, most of the time we don't hear that answer. Unfortunately, too many of us have parents who don't make us feel as if we belong. Unfortunately, we belong to a society that prioritizes all the wrong things—things like money and fame and attractiveness and overall status—forcing us to judge ourselves against all the wrong standards, standards by which we always come up short. So then we find ourselves alone in the darkness, where the voices come for us and tell us how stupid and ugly and worthless we are.

But it's a lie. It's a fuckin' lie. You belong here simply because you *are* here. God created every single one of us with our own inherent worth and value and dignity. Mental illness is the lie that undermines that truth.

In fact, not only is it a lie; it's a lie that begets more lies in turn, as lies often do. One of the most insidious of those lies is that your problems are yours alone. Because you've never been inside someone else's head to feel the pain they feel, you're convinced that you're the only person suffering like this—that you're the only person who has *ever* suffered like this. Which is why you can be surrounded by friends and family telling you, "It's okay," and still feel so horribly alone. It's also why the situation feels so hopeless. Why even ask for help when nobody could possibly help you? Because if you're the only one with this problem, what are the chances of doctors ever diagnosing and treating you? You're so broken that no one will ever be able to find the cure.

Of course, none of that is true. There are millions of people who hurt the same way that you hurt. There are thousands of doctors and therapists who understand how to treat you and how to help you. But you can't see that because the thing that you're sick with comes with an absence of hope, an absence of faith—the inability to see yourself and your life clearly.

Have you ever asked someone for help? Why or why not?

Have you talked to other people about your fears? Have you found people experiencing the same feelings and struggles as you?

DAY 4

Stuck

When in a state of major turmoil, I fall into this place where the minutiae of life will bury me. I'll have a hard time making decisions, even about the smallest things. I think there are two broad categories of anxious people: those who are anxious about things that they can't control, and those who are anxious about the things they can.

With major events outside my control, such as getting hit by a truck on the freeway, I've always had a much easier time being like, *Well, okay, it is what it is.* I've always been far more anxious about what I *can* control. I get stuck trying to figure out the perfect way to do the thing and I think, *Don't fuck this up. Don't fuck this up. Don't fuck this up.* The thing *has* to be perfect, because if a thing is not perfect, it's a failure, and failures don't receive love. And why do I think this way? Because that's the way I was programmed as a kid by my parents.

Your childhood is baggage that you're forced to carry around your entire life—that's why it is important to get help with your baggage. I am lucky to have friends who care about me. When everything feels meaningless they remind me, "It's okay!" Don't let yourself stay stuck. Don't allow yourself to believe that failure is your final destination. You're going to fuck up, but you can learn from those mistakes. You *can* take control and get unstuck.

When was the last time you felt stuck? What was going on? What lies were you believing?

Did you reach out to someone for help? What can you do differently next time you are stuck?

DAY 5

Be Open

Even though our knowledge of the human mind and body has increased a thousandfold over time, and miraculous breakthroughs of understanding do occur, many of the mysteries of existence remain beyond our grasp. We're constantly revising what we know about what we don't know. All throughout history, scientists have said, "We've got it! We've figured it out!" Then a few years go by, and it turns out everyone's assumptions were wrong. We grew up thinking that dinosaurs were these enormous reptiles. Then one day all the paleontologists said, "Well, it turns out they were more like enormous chickens." Nowhere is this truer than with mental health.

Mental illness is a subject that we don't talk about enough, that we don't understand enough, that we're scared to confront. In many cases, we're so ignorant we don't even know how much we don't know. My friends knew I was struggling, but they didn't fully grasp the depths of what I was struggling with. They wanted to help me and support me, but most of what I heard from them was, "You seem unhappy." And I was unhappy, deeply unhappy. But none of them could put a finger on why, and neither could I. I'd been in and out of therapy a few times in my life, addressing symptoms here and there, doing little hit-and-runs—as they call them—on my various issues. But I'd never fully digested and metabolized what I needed to know in order to cope with all my pain and sadness and anger.

I realized that—more than anything—I needed to be open. Open to the idea that it was okay to discuss my struggles. Open to the idea that I wasn't alone. Open to the idea that I needed to work through the pain that I continuously pushed down. Open to the idea of eventually being okay.

Have you struggled with being open? What struggles caused you to be unhappy?

How can you talk more? What can you do to confront the things you're scared of?

DAY 6

We Don't Know

I reached a point where I knew that I needed professional help if I wanted to stay alive. With my sister's support, I decided to fly out to a place in Connecticut and check myself in. I didn't know what I didn't know. I didn't know what I was going to get out of it, and I didn't know who I was going to be on the other side of it. I was afraid I would turn into a version of myself that I didn't like. Part of me was afraid that because this wasn't a spiritual facility, I would come out of my experience with even less faith and less spirit than when I went in. I was so lost, all I knew for certain was that I wanted someone to tell me what the fuck was going on, to give me an answer, a capital-D diagnosis.

That is what many of us, wrongly, have come to expect from medicine and science. The truth, especially with mental health, is that there are still so many big questions to be answered— questions that get harder to address the more hubris we have in believing we understand them. We started out in a world where mental conditions like depression and schizophrenia were chalked up to sorcery and demons and witchcraft. Then it was Freud, and everything was about dreams and wanting to sleep with your mother. Then it was B. F. Skinner and behaviorism, where there's no free will and no human soul and we're all bodies with nerve endings driven by stimulus-response mechanisms that seek to maximize pleasure and avoid pain.

For me, the most important and influential of these figures is Carl Jung, whom I consider the originator of the idea of radical acceptance—recognizing the darkness in yourself in order to understand the darkness in others. But the reality is that everyone is making their best guess. Nobody knows everything for sure. All of us should put our hands in the air and say, "We've been so fuckin' wrong about so many things, and all we want is to learn more to get closer to the truth." Ideally, we should want to know everything that affects us in every possible way. We should want to be the healthiest, strongest version of ourselves and go make the world a better place, and to do that, it's important to use mental and spiritual and emotional exercises to dig into that stuff. Too often in life we pick a point on the horizon and say, "That's where I need to be, and all I need is the shortest route between here and there." But that's wrong. We have to accept that we don't always know where we're going and that we don't even know how to get there. We have to be open to the journey. We have to be open to discovery.

Are you open to the unknown journey of
life and the discovery that lies ahead?

Why do you think society is unwilling to accept and
acknowledge that they don't know everything?
How can you make efforts in your own life to be
more honest with acceptance and not knowing?

DAY 7

Faith

Have you ever questioned whether God exists? I know believers will come at you and say that you shouldn't question His existence. When I was in a treatment facility in Connecticut, losing my faith in God had hit me so hard. My whole life I've been adamant that there is, there *has to be*, some form of objective truth. Some objective truths are obvious, like gravity. Gravity doesn't need you to believe in it in order for it to work. It's gravity. It just works. But there are other truths, too, such as "It's better to be kind than not be kind." To me that's objective truth. It's a universal principle. The difference is you *do* have to believe that being kind is better than not being kind in order to see that it works. You have to manifest it in your actions. But people don't always treat those types of truths as universal. "Everything's relative," they say, and everything that cannot be scientifically proven or measured gets put into this category of "Well, that's your truth and this is my truth." Which has always driven me completely insane, because applying subjectivity erodes the objectivity of hard, constant, actual truth.

One of the issues I started to work out in Connecticut is where this rigidity of mine came from. I think in large part it has to do with my not being parented in a healthy or productive way. My mother in particular was so volatile; I was forever in a state of trying to figure out which side of her was going to be on display in any given moment and how I was supposed to relate to her. *There has to be an answer to this riddle,* young Zac would tell himself subconsciously. *There has to be a correct way to behave that solves this problem and keeps me away from the wrath and insanity of my mom.* So I became obsessed with finding it.

Ultimately, in the absence of proper parenting, I found those rules and that truth in God, in the Bible. "This is the handbook," I was taught. "These are God's step-by-step instructions for living a good and worthy life." Amazing. Wonderful. I'll take that. And that sustained me for a long time. But when my faith crumbled, I was at a complete loss for how to orient myself in a world with no objective truth.

Do you find yourself struggling with objective truths and universal principles? How do you come to terms with the outcomes that both ideals present?

What do you do every day to maintain your faith in God and deepen your relationship with Him?

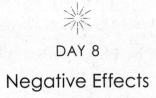

DAY 8

Negative Effects

To understand the root of all my struggles with mental health, picture a glass of water. It's sitting on the kitchen counter, glistening with condensation as the ice inside it crackles and melts on a hot summer day. Six years old and all rambunctious and sweaty from running around in the yard, I run into the house to get a drink, and I accidentally knock the glass over and it shatters across the kitchen floor.

Now, if I knock that glass over and my mom is in a good mood, she'll turn from whatever she's doing and say, sweet as can be, "Oh, honey, it's okay. Don't worry about it. We can get another glass." But if I knock that glass over and she's in a bad mood, she'll turn on me and scream, *"Look what you did, you little shit! What the fuck is wrong with you?! You fucking idiot!"*

That was my mother: rational, kind, and loving—or irrational, volatile, and lashing out in anger at the slightest provocation. Living with her was like living with Jekyll and Hyde, and on any given day, my sisters and I had no idea which way she was going to go, what would set her off, or how far it would escalate. The glass of water could be anything: a fight with my sisters, a bad grade on a test, playing the radio too loud. It could be something supremely important or something completely trivial; it didn't matter. We were forever walking on eggshells and dodging trip mines. Throw in her ever-increasing alcohol dependency and the slowly deteriorating codependent relationship with my equally broken and abusive stepdad, and the rest of the script writes itself. It wasn't unusual to come home to find all of my stepdad's shit on the front lawn because my mom had decided to throw it out there. It was just as typical to come home and find all my mom's shit out on the lawn because my stepdad had decided it was his turn to do the same. There was nothing remarkable or special about any of it. Coming home to some kind of emotional Armageddon was like, "Oh, it's Tuesday."

My sisters and I were being traumatized, plain and simple. It wasn't blunt-force physical trauma; we weren't getting beaten by our parents, thank God, but we were getting psychologically KO'd on a daily basis. For the longest time, I didn't know that it was abnormal. I assumed that this was how everybody's parents were, that this was how human beings operated. And because I thought it was normal, I couldn't see the negative effects it was having or how those negative effects were accumulating and compounding in my head, year after year after year. Once I became an adult, I couldn't see the ways in which I still approached every aspect of my life the way I did that glass of water: terrified that anything other than perfection would trigger an onslaught of pain and abuse and rejection.

If you were abused as a child, did you think the
abusive behavior was normal? If you were abused,
at what point did you realize it wasn't normal?

In what ways has your childhood influenced your
perception of perfection and rejection?

DAY 9
Dig Deep

Emotional trauma can be generational, passed down from parent to child like a family heirloom. You carry it with you and it's
not even yours.

If you found yourself suffering from a debilitating condition like heart disease or breast cancer, what's one of the first
things you would do? You'd go to your family tree. You'd look

back to see where it mostly likely came from in order to narrow down the root causes and the best course of treatment. With the advances in DNA analysis we have now, it's amazing what science can do. Mental health is no different. The root causes are all there. You just have to go looking for them. Needless to say, not every trauma or condition is linked to family. You may suffer from trauma at work or be in an abusive relationship, but if your story is anything like mine, a lot of your answers are tucked away with the skeletons in the family closet.

Trying to figure out your family history is a journey, and a tough one at that. Getting people to open up about the trauma they've endured is not an easy thing to do. People are often unwilling to talk. Or, if they do talk, they're unwilling to be honest. Everyone is doing their best to frame the past the way they want to see it, which is not necessarily the way that it actually was. Still, you do the best you can. You become a bit of an archaeologist. You search and you dig, and ultimately you piece together facts and form conclusions from the best evidence you can gather. Which is why you start by telling your own story. You regurgitate all the unhealthy patterns and behaviors you witnessed and endured over the years, and that at least gives you a place to start. But the cool thing is that by understanding psychology more, by going to therapy more, by learning about yourself more, you in turn learn so much about your parents and your family—and the world, for that matter.

Have you addressed the trauma that's linked to your family? What have you discovered?

Set aside time and retell your story. Write it down, talk to a friend, or say it aloud to yourself. It might seem awkward, but this will be a way you can learn more about yourself and your family.

DAY 10

Rewrite Your Ending

You are not yourself. You are the story you tell yourself about yourself. And as the author of that story, you have the power to rewrite the ending.

Human beings love stories. Books, podcasts, television shows, movies—we devour them. It's something that's universal across cultures. It's been a constant from the days of tribal peoples recounting their greatest adventures on cave walls up to the latest streaming series you're watching on your phone. It's the reason why Hollywood is the global behemoth it is. It's the reason why actors like me have the job that we do. We exist to tell stories.

If you've never stopped to ask yourself why, the answer is because the human brain is wired for it. We are storytelling animals because stories are the mechanism through which we store and process information. Think about what happens when someone asks you where you were born. You might give them a one-word answer, but more than likely you're going to tell them your origin story: the town where you were born, why your parents lived there at the time, what your parents did, how long you lived there before you moved away, why you moved away, and so on. Because all those facts are stored in a narrative sequence, and it is the narrative sequence that gives the facts meaning. A good story takes a fact and gives it direction and momentum—a trajectory. The stories we tell ourselves communally, the myths and legends spun by political leaders and others, become the organizing forces of the culture that shapes us as a society, for good and for ill. Meanwhile, the personal stories we tell ourselves about ourselves become the dominant forces that shape how we perceive our own lives, also for good and for ill.

What are the stories you retell often?

Are you stuck believing your ending is already written?
What steps can you take to rewrite your ending?

DAY 11

Not So Different

When you're lost in the depths of depression or spiraling out of control with anxiety, part of what makes you feel so hopeless and lost is the feeling that you're all alone and nobody could possibly understand your pain because nobody has ever suffered the way that you are suffering in that moment. But that isn't true. Not only are people across the world suffering in the same way you're suffering; people have suffered in the exact same way you're suffering since the dawn of civilization.

Life on earth today may look nothing like it did thousands of years ago. Mankind's technological advancements may have remade the planet in ways unimaginable to our ancestors. But the core of what it is to be human has, arguably, remained a constant. We can still look to ancient texts from all manner of different civilizations, and maybe not all of it is up to date, but many of the basic lessons of how our personalities work and how to be a good person and live a meaningful life still apply. It's merely the setting that's different.

Seen in that context, the struggles we endure today are not some kind of unique torture being visited upon us because of our own failing. Quite the opposite. They're universal, timeless. The thing that you're wrestling with? Someone in ancient Sumer was wrestling with that exact same thing five thousand years ago. Which is comforting, or at least it should be, because it means you're not alone. It also means that, just maybe, somebody's already figured you out.

What are you wrestling with right now? Do you know other people in your own life who have or are wrestling with the same situation?

DAY 12

Our Gifts

Ultimately, society cannot function if we're not using our gifts for the good of the whole. There's a reason we are all different hues of this spectrum. We're all a part of the same light, but we each serve a different purpose. We're all interconnected and linked to each other. We balance each other. We need each other. There is no right way to be. Not everyone can be the Reformer; not everyone can be the Helper; we are all complementing one another to make a better world.

My life coach thought it would be helpful for me to understand my story and my personality through the context of the Enneagram, and she was right. It might not be the right diagnostic tool for everyone; there are countless other ways to define and categorize the different types of human personalities. But I found it incredibly helpful and fascinating.

When you take an Enneagram test, it doesn't tell you exactly what number you are. It gives you an array of highest probabilities, but it still requires you to do the work to read through all of the chapters and see which one resonates with you. When you read the chapters about the personality types in the Enneagram, you tend to think that you could be several different types, because there's a great deal of overlap. But then you get to the one chapter that nails you, and you almost feel naked when you're reading it. It exposes you and all your tricks. That's how I felt when I sat down and read the chapter on type 7, the Enthusiast. It was like reading my mail, all of my mail: good mail, bad mail, all of it.

Oh God, I thought, *this is* me.

And it was. The primary role of the Enthusiast is to bring joy. That is their gift to bring to the world. But accompanying that is the Enthusiast's primary need: their shadow motivation. You see, the desire to bring joy is coupled with the need to avoid pain. That is the true definition of the archetype, and that fit me like a glove. I was drawn to the world of entertainment practically from the womb. As I had grown up with a single mom in Ventura, I found television was a huge part of my life. It was the babysitter, the constant companion. I probably learned most of what I knew about life—or what I thought life was supposed to be—from watching TV. It was my first exposure to families

29

that were "healthy" or "normal." We never watched *Leave It to Beaver* or *Father Knows Best* or any of those shows, the ones with the archetypal happy, suburban, nuclear families. For us it was always TGIF: *Full House* or *Step by Step* or *Family Matters*, and to the extent that those families were a bit more dysfunctional than the Cleavers, they were always dysfunctional in a "Ha ha, let's all joke and laugh our way through it" type of way, which probably didn't help all that much if you really stop to think about it.

Have you taken the Enneagram? If yes, what's your type? If not, there's no time like the present. Take the test.

Coping Mechanisms

My mother learned to abuse in order to show that she was abused. All of my mom's temper tantrums and her self-destructive behavior was an attempt to shout out to the world, "Don't you see? Don't you see how much pain I'm in? Don't you see what this horrible woman did to me?" But the world couldn't see it, so the world never acknowledged it, so my mom's abuse continued.

It not only continued, by the way; it escalated. Over time, always being right was no longer the ticket to being loved; always being right was the surefire way to drive off the people she needed to give her the love she so sorely lacked. Over time, my mother's ability to inflict pain on us diminished because we were developing our own unhealthy coping mechanisms to protect ourselves against her. Our synapses and neural pathways were frantically rewiring themselves, creating subconscious behaviors that would help us avoid trauma and seek out pleasure and love in our own dysfunctional, self-destructive ways. My sisters and I stayed away from her; we threw ourselves into unhealthy relationships with other people and our different obsessions.

And so, over time, as my mother was less and less able to diffuse her pain by inflicting it on others, she turned more and more to dulling the pain inside herself by self-medicating.

Do you know someone who inflicts
their pain onto others?

Has someone inflicted their pain on you? What coping
mechanisms did you use to deal with the pain?

DAY 14

When I Grow Up

I can remember watching HBO with my sisters, and I'm talking about the OG HBO: the logo flying in and the whooshing lights swirling inside the *O* and that big theme song blaring out of the TV, "*Da-na-na, na-na, na-na-na-na!*" It was the best. We'd sit there, no grown-ups present, and watch whatever was on, anything and everything; I watched *The Terminator* on HBO when I was like four years old. My parents didn't know, or didn't care. They weren't around. As long as we were occupied and not burning the house down, hey, knock yourself out.

At that age I had no idea what being an actor was, or how a television show was made, but I can remember, very distinctly, at the age of four, becoming cognizant of the idea that I could intentionally make people laugh. I learned that I could mimic people's voices and personalities, and do weird, silly gags, and it would make people smile. I started learning dumb kid jokes and I would tell them all the time. Once I'd achieved the laugh, I knew that I'd accomplished something. Because a laughing person is a happy person. I had created joy where joy hadn't existed before, and that felt like a superpower—a superpower that gave me purpose in life.

I was the middle boy between two sisters. It was my mom; my two sisters; my two aunts; my cousin Nikki, who was like our third sister; and my grandma. I was floating in a sea of estrogen. Our family outings were going to JCPenney—or Nordstrom or Macy's or Marshalls, or all of them—and shopping. As the middle kid and the only boy, I was always fighting to have a voice and identity of my own and constantly creating worlds of my own imagination. The television and the video games I played through the television became the worlds that I lived in and loved. I wanted to emulate them and be a part of them.

When I was around six, I started becoming aware of how the whole mechanism of entertainment worked. That's a television, and those are actors, and the camera is here, and the set is over there, and so on. That's when it dawned on me, *Oh, okay, this thing where I create laughter and joy in people, I can do that as a job?* And that was it. Something inside me clicked, and from that point on there was no turning back. I loved people, loved making them happy, and I put all of my eggs in that basket.

As a child did you ever have an aha moment and
know what you wanted to be when you grew up?

Did you ever want to be more than one thing? If so,
what professions were you interested in pursuing?

DAY 15

Pain

Pain is necessary. It is your mind and your body telling you, *Hey!
There's something happening to you that you need to deal with.* For the
longest time, I didn't realize that I needed to experience my pain.
I needed to digest it, metabolize it, and understand it. I never
stopped to let myself feel it. I was always under the impression
that to let myself do that would be wallowing in misery and self-
pity, which is always a potential danger. But there's also a healthy

need to sit with your pain long enough to process it. Once you have, you can go, "Okay, I've mourned it. I've seen the way it's affecting me. I've learned the lessons I need to learn from it. I've made my peace with it, and now I can move on from it." Oftentimes, we have a hard time doing that. We're always racing to get ahead of the pain, and because we're so fucking good at creating joy, we always have the ability to stay one step ahead of it.

Until we don't.

I am an Enthusiast. When you're an Enthusiast and you are not in a good or healthy place, you don't merely avoid pain by spreading joy to others. You avoid pain by numbing it—and the best way to numb it is through the "fun" of gluttony. Gluttony is the result of Enthusiasts abusing and indulging their gifts in unhealthy ways. We want the highest level of that intensity and that enthusiasm and the joy of the ever-growing, nonstop party in order to run away from the pain. And that, too, is me.

Pain is a part of life. It comes in waves and, sometimes, seasons. In order to fully enjoy the life you're given, you must process pain. It isn't self-pity or self-loathing. It is a part of your quest for peace and happiness.

What pain have you suppressed? How can
you begin working through that pain?

What painful experience has made you a stronger person?

DAY 16

Experience Everything

I have always struggled with FOMO. I've always had a hard time
when someone says, "Hey, we're doing a thing on Friday, want
to come?" I struggle to commit to that party because, for all I
know, between now and Friday something else may come up,
and it's going to be way cooler than whatever this thing is, and
I don't want to put myself in the corner committing to what this
is going to be and losing out. It's the same reason why I struggle

so much at the ice cream shop. I have a hard time deciding which ice cream to pick, because if I choose one, I can't have the others. That has happened to me my entire life. I thought I was just getting overwhelmed with options, but the reality was that I wanted to experience *everything*.

All through my high school and community theater years, I wasn't exactly living on the straight and narrow. I'm not so sure you could say that the jocks partied harder than the theater nerds. The merriment we had probably put a lot of the football players to shame. It was not healthy. I was getting high with my buddies every day. We'd find each other every afternoon and say, "Who's got the weed?" And then one of us would get the weed and we'd go get lit. At the time, I thought I was just having fun; I didn't realize how much I was self-medicating to compensate for all the trauma I was experiencing at home.

You may be able to bring joy to others while self-medicating, but you may well be dulling your gifts and potentially wasting them in self-indulgence. Focusing your gift on indulging yourself is, in the end, a masturbatory practice of ever-diminishing returns. Eventually the noise of the party will no longer drown out the pain. You don't ever get healthy, and the hole inside you never gets filled. That hole can only ever be filled by sharing your gifts with the world, fulfilling your purpose and becoming your higher self—a person who is in communion with your community, your Creator, and all of creation.

There's the old saying that "Your greatest strength is your greatest weakness." The dichotomy of bringing joy and avoiding pain fits that pretty well. But I think a lot of people miss an important point. The armor we create for ourselves, the coping mechanism we use to protect ourselves, can be the very thing that's hurting us in the long run *even as* it's propping us up in the short run.

Do you struggle with FOMO? Have you always had an issue with it?

Have you created armor recently? If so, what steps can you take to remove the armor?

DAY 17

Just Be

Talk to anyone who's been through depression or some major mental illness, and one phrase you're likely to hear over and over again is, "And that was the only thing that got me through it." It's what gets you out of bed in the morning. You're a farmer and you have to grow food for your community. You're a parent and you've got a kid who needs to eat breakfast and get to school. We are all, in our own way, searching for that one thing.

Part of poor mental health is not loving yourself, not valuing yourself. We're all walking around this little blue dot floating in space, saying, "Who am I? What am I doing here? What are all of you doing here? What is the meaning of life?" That is the human condition. But anytime you feel that your life has a purpose, you can feel that you're here for a reason, whatever that reason is. Believing that you are here for a reason is a way to feel valuable and therefore worthy of being loved, which can be the thing that carries you through any season of darkness. When I was going through the darkness of my marriage, my ex-wife's dog was often the only source of motivation for me to get out of bed. There was another life that I had to go attend to. I had a purpose, even if it was a small one. Otherwise I'd just lay there with my mind spinning around, going, *I made an irrevocable mistake. I fucked it all up. What's the point of even going on living?*

A lot of us find our purpose and we think that finding our purpose is the thing that gives us value. It's the answer to the Big Question. "Why was I put here? I was put here to do this thing." But I don't know that that's the case. I think that most enlightened people you meet will tell you that's not true. I think the why of existence is merely to be. Your value and your worth as a human being are not connected to anything that you do or accomplish in the material world. All that you have to do is be. Just be.

What did you do today? How are you choosing to be?

List three things you love about yourself.

Patterns

Without even knowing it, we can spend our whole lives stuck in feedback loops, repeating the same patterns of behavior, stuck in the same narrative we've told ourselves about ourselves. In many cases those patterns and narratives can be positive ones, but in cases where they're negative or self-destructive, we have to learn to recognize them in order to short-circuit them and reset them, like doing a hard reboot on your computer's operating system.

Part of my mental health journey included learning about dialectic behavioral therapy, or DBT. It's a form of therapy that helps you understand the cause-and-effect mechanisms of the emotions and thought patterns that trigger certain unhealthy behaviors in your life. It helps you identify those thought patterns so you can see when you're getting caught in them in order to short-circuit them and correct them with healthier behaviors. It's very practical, almost like math. There are actual exercises and worksheets that you can do.

For example, whenever X happens, your anxiety starts spinning out of control and you start imagining all the worst-case scenarios of your life. Then you get wrapped up in those imagined realities and you start stressing yourself out over possibilities that don't even exist and will likely never happen. DBT steps in and says, "Okay, let's back up. Let's identify X. What is X? When you start to experience X, instead of going off in a death spiral of anxiety and stress, what's something you can do to help yourself feel better? A calming piece of music, maybe, or a breathing exercise." It's almost like in *Inception* where you have a totem that serves as your anchor to bring you back to reality where you feel safe and at home.

DBT is a way of acknowledging what has been said by many philosophers and psychologists for some time: You are not the voice in your head. You're the one who hears it. It's insane how our brains work, with all these synapses firing and different thoughts running through our minds all the time, some of them healthy, many of them not. Half the time you think something and go, "Where did that come from?" You are not controlling it, and you need to recognize it by saying something like, "What I'm currently thinking is not even close to real. It's not even something that I want to be real. It's my imagination running wild, and

I've started manufacturing a false reality based on my imagination and not on true reality." It's about establishing a baseline of truth and then constantly reminding yourself of that baseline and bringing yourself back to it.

Do you experience emotions very intensely?
How do you think DBT could help you?

To learn more about DBT, check out this resource: https://dbtselfhelp.com/

You Are Worthy

It would be better if we all let go of the notion that we need to have purpose to feel worthy of love. I think that we all have a difficult time truly accepting that we are exactly who we are meant to be and that we don't need to be doing anything else to earn or be worthy of that love. Even if you have no social connection to others and aren't capable of doing anything constructive at this exact moment, you still possess the infinite value of being a human soul in the universe. You're still worthy of receiving God's love. You *are* God's love. We are, all of us, extensions of the Creator's life, light, and love. This I believe with all my heart.

In the Old Testament in Exodus 3, Moses said to God, "What's your name?" and God said, "I am." I think that is one of the most profound passages ever written in any manuscript, whether you're a Christian, a Jew, a Muslim, or whatever. You have the entity that we call God not giving itself any proper name or noun. But rather, it declares that *it is.* This passage is saying *sooo* many things, but one of the most profound is that God is not attaching any value to some title that may define Him. God is declaring His infinite and all-connecting presence. A presence that we are all extensions of. But we ignore that, and we all run around trying to find some purpose to give our lives meaning when in fact our lives have meaning simply because we have them.

Do you struggle with feeling worthy of love?

How does it make you feel knowing that you're worthy of receiving God's love? If you are struggling to believe that, what can you do to gently remind yourself each day of this truth?

DAY 20

Stand Up for Yourself

Trauma breeds trauma. I've lived it. My mother was abusive. She wore down my dad, my stepdad, my sisters, and me. There was a time when I decided enough was enough. I stopped talking to my mother because it wasn't healthy for me. Then a friend of the family begrudgingly convinced me to talk to her in the spirit of Thanksgiving. So I did.

I have to say, I was a bit stunned. By that point in my life, there was little my mother could say or do that surprised me. Then, after a heated confrontation, she said, "You know what, Zachary? I'd be happier today if you were *dead*."

This was a new low even for her.

But the thing about my mom's tirades was that she was all bark and no bite, and I knew that. I knew she didn't actually want me dead. This was just her extremely unhealthy way of trying to get people to recognize her pain and cater to it. Still, this needed to stop.

My first instinct was to somehow document that this was happening. My mom was a queen of never admitting to something when she was called on it. My whole life, whenever she said horrible shit, you could quote it back to her verbatim two hours later, and she'd say, "I *never* said that." We all knew the tactic; it was part of the crazy-making, part of the gaslighting. Eventually, you'd be second-guessing yourself, like, *Wait, did she say it?* And she was always so overboard in her denial that eventually you'd say, "Fuck it, it's not even worth it. I'm not even going to deal. I'm not going down that road." So nobody could ever hold her accountable.

But that day, when she said she'd be happier if I were dead, I had the presence of mind to know that if I didn't get it on the record, she was going to say that it had never happened. If smartphones had existed then, I would have whipped one out and recorded her, but since I didn't have that, the next best thing was to have my stepdad and family friend, Adam, as witnesses. So I looked at her and said, "Mom, I want you to say that one more time, so we're all clear. I want you to say exactly what you just said."

She stopped cold. I could see the anger and fear in her eyes. She either had to acknowledge that what she said was out of line and apologize *or* she had to repeat one of the most vile things that she'd ever said to one of her own children and then actually try and stand by it. I could see her thinking, *Do I double down on this? Or do I admit that I was wrong?* Unfortunately, being wrong still equaled being unlovable in the twisted neural pathways of my mother's incredible brain. So she took a deep breath, looked me dead in the eye, and said, "I'd be happier today if you were dead."

"Mom," I said, "I love you, but I will never be spoken to like that ever again. I'm going to go now. I want us to be good with each other, but it's going to require some serious therapy to get us there. From now on I will only speak to you in the presence of a professional who can help us. You guys pick the counselor. I'll pay for the counselor. I love you, and goodbye."

Then I stood up and walked out.

Have you stood up for yourself and told a family member you could no longer continue the relationship? How did they react? Did you feel emotionally safe after drawing the line?

DAY 21

Tracing Inner Narratives

My dialectic behavioral therapist at the therapy facility in Connecticut had a kind of East Coast New York vibe to her. She was a no-nonsense, cut-the-bullshit type of person. She was cool. She was one of my favorites. She was one of the people who I felt was more on my wavelength. I liked her approach to DBT because it was very direct. Like the life coaching, it was the opposite of the weepy, Kleenexy approach of psychotherapy.

To me, DBT was almost like a form of parenting, the way parents talk to a child—or, the way parents *should* talk to a child—when the child is freaking out about something that only exists in the child's mind. The parent goes, "Whoa, come sit down. Let's walk through it. Calm down, calm down. Breathe. Okay. We're in a boat. I know you think we're going to sink, but the boat is sturdy. The captain knows what he's doing. We have life preservers and life rafts. We're going to be fine." You have to walk a child between what is real and what's fantasy because when we're kids our imaginations are big and out of control at times.

In my life, probably the most self-destructive feedback loop, the most debilitating inner narrative that I'd been living out, over and over again like my own personal *Groundhog Day*, was in my relationships with women. When I first arrived in Connecticut, I was still devastated about the woman I'd broken up with when I moved to Austin. The way I saw it, I'd ruined my life by letting her go. To help me understand how the end of that relationship was not the end of my world but simply another iteration of a pattern, my therapist went to the beginning of my relationship history to help me break that pattern down.

What is the most debilitating inner narrative you're living out? If you've worked through a negative narrative in the past, what was it?

Have you ever broken down the origin and patterns of a bad inner narrative? If so, what did you learn?

Hit Bottom

One of the most gut-wrenching decisions you have to make about helping someone is knowing when to stop helping them. Letting someone you love hit bottom is a difficult thing to do. It's *rough*, because if you decide to let them go, there's always the risk you might lose them forever.

You hear "hitting bottom" a lot in addiction and recovery circles. Based on my own experience, hitting bottom means coming to the end of yourself, being truly humbled and on your knees. We all have tricks and tools and schemes that we use to navigate this world. Even as our problems mount and our circumstances deteriorate, we tell ourselves lies about how we're the ones doing the right thing, that we're playing the game and playing it well and all our problems are someone else's fault.

Hitting bottom is when all those tricks and tools and schemes have stopped working. Hitting bottom is when all the things you've used to prop yourself up in the past, whether it's drugs or sex or alcohol, simply don't do anything to erase the pain anymore. Hitting bottom is the moment when you can no longer lie to yourself, when the scales fall from your eyes and you have to confront the truth about who you are and the pain that you've caused yourself and others. I had hit bottom when I moved to Austin where, after thirty-seven years of self-medicating and white-knuckling my way through so many seasons of anxiety and depression, I finally had to admit I was wrong about so many things and that I desperately needed help.

In most cases, a person must hit bottom so they can recognize they need help or take a step toward recovery. It's hard, but you must start from the bottom to build yourself up.

When did you hit rock bottom? How did you build yourself up?

What major changes did you make after you hit rock bottom?

DAY 23

Enabling

Many people have the presence of mind to seek or accept help well before they get anywhere near hitting bottom. I was not one of those people. Neither was my mom. For decades, she'd been navigating life with all her tricks and tools and schemes, barely staying afloat, drinking to dull the pain, hitting the clearance sales to get her little dopamine boosts. Ultimately, the thing that kept her from cratering completely was having enablers—family and friends who she could consistently depend on to either forgive or forget her transgressions, allowing her to never fully feel the consequences that should have come with her actions. Nobody had ever let her hit bottom. At a certain point, helping becomes enabling, and we were already well past that point when my mom was caught committing federal mail tampering and identity theft to try to get out of a DUI arrest.

In the years after a holiday blowout, I'd kept up a firm boundary between my mom and myself. Most of that time I managed to maintain a reasonably healthy relationship with my stepfather, Gary. Then, at a certain point, he started asking for money, which I knew would happen because my mom was horrible with money. No matter how much Gary made, she would find a way to spend it all. I helped with some of the bills in months they were behind. I also gave them a car. I did it because I thought it was my responsibility, until I realized it wasn't. Children are not responsible for their parents. Yes, we should be there when they're elderly and infirm, but it's not our job to be there when they are acting like children refusing to be responsible for themselves. I eventually made it clear I wouldn't give them more money until we all went to counseling and my mom got help for her financial problems.

Have you ever been part of an enabling situation? How can you prevent yourself from enabling a loved one?

Have other people enabled you to prevent you from hitting rock bottom? How did you handle it?

Check Your Ego

I believe that we as human beings are infinitely valuable—and entirely unimportant. We are infinitely small specks of sand in an infinitely large mosaic of infinitely small specks of sand. If you can grasp that, then your ego can let go of your pride, your hubris, and your fear. You will be ready to say, "It's not about me. The world's not about me. But my world is about me. I am about me, and I will love me."

The ego is a fascinating thing, and it has one prime function: survival. It's tied directly to our sympathetic nervous system, which is what kicks on when we feel threatened—our modes of fight, flight, or freeze. Its goal is to protect you at all costs. It will do anything it has to do to get you safely into bed each night. A healthy ego, responding to everyday challenges, does so in a perfectly normal way. You encounter a setback or challenge in life, and a mature ego helps you assert yourself calmly and confidently in order to solve the problem. But an immature ego falls back into the most extreme versions of survival. Every "threat" is met with a response similar to that of our most primitive selves. A simple daily challenge could be seen and felt like a lion stalking you on the savanna. Your ego kicks into fight-or-flight mode, and you do everything you can to avoid confronting the lion because the lion is going to eat you.

For a child, still developing and still unformed, an abusive mother like mine is a lion on the savanna. Only you can't run away from her. She's your mother. So what your ego does is create all manner of defense mechanisms that allow you to evade and deflect and absorb the fear and the pain that you feel. I think of the ego as being like your armor, or an exoskeleton. It's shielding us. When trauma comes along and smacks you, your ego takes the blow. It may teach you to repress negative feelings and memories. It may teach you to take the anger you feel toward your abusive parent and displace it by bullying yourself or others. These coping mechanisms are unhealthy and bad, but our ego is doing them for the right reason: to protect us. In the short term, they help us. In the long run, not so much.

Can you think of a time you reacted to a "threat" in an immature way? How would you handle that situation now?

How does your ego protect you? What are some ways you can cope in a healthier way?

DAY 25

Hard Truth

The single biggest defense mechanism my ego created for me was in my work. I found entertainment as a way of survival. As an adolescent, throwing myself into high school and community theater gave me a place where I felt safe and protected and appreciated. I could go out onstage every night and create joy in a hundred smiling faces. Then, after the curtain fell, I got to go out and party surrounded by my friends who loved me and supported me. It was great. It protected me. It *worked*. Every time I felt pain, or was even afraid that I might feel pain, my body knew what to do: Get onstage. Create joy. Call a bunch of friends. Throw a party. Self-medicate. Rinse. Repeat.

I learned to follow that script to the letter. It became so ingrained in who I was that I forgot it was something I had learned—and could therefore unlearn. And you have to unlearn it at some point, because at some point it stops working. The ego, for all it does to protect you, can also be insanely crippling. Because every blow to your armor leaves a mark—a dent here and a crinkle there. As the years pass, you're walking around thinking that you're still pretty smooth and intact, but you're not. You're relying more and more on this armor that's completely cracked and warped and misshapen. Inside that armor, you're not standing tall and hale and healthy. You're all bent and warped and misshapen too.

The hard truth that I've learned is that your ego can protect you for only so long, and it can never actually heal you. Indeed, it becomes an impediment to the healing you need. The only way to get where you ultimately need to go is to not rely on your ego anymore. You have to shed your armor and stand naked and exposed and confront the pain and the trauma that you've been running from. Only then will you find healing and enlightenment and peace.

The stronger your ego is, the harder it is to let it go. I had, and still have, one hell of an ego. That fucker is strong. To endure all the childhood abuse that I did and still make it all the way to my late thirties without the slightest awareness of how damaged I was? That's some industrial-grade armor plating right there. But ultimately, in the end, it failed me, particularly when it came to the one area where it had given me the most support: my work.

Has your ego prevented you from healing?

What coping mechanism does your ego turn to?
How can you approach things in a healthier way?

DAY 26

Inhumanity

Hollywood is not community theater, not by a long shot. The scripts that I learned to follow in my youth didn't necessarily translate when I moved from one to the other. Arriving in Los Angeles and seeing so much inefficiency and inhumanity on display, I couldn't believe the way that the system worked—or, rather, didn't work. Maybe it's because of the environment I was raised in, but ever since I was a kid, born with this particular head and this particular heart, I have been constantly driven to evaluate systems and institutions, to deconstruct them, to figure out what works and what doesn't and why it works or doesn't work. It's why I was so obsessed with that book *The Way Things Work*, which broke down different machines to show how they functioned inside. Which can be maddening, to be honest, because you aren't satisfied a lot of the time with how and why things are done.

Because of my engineer's mind and my empathetic heart, I've always bucked when I feel like something is broken to the point where it's inhumane, or inefficient, which are often one and the same. The engineer in me associates inefficiency with inhumanity, because anything that's inefficient wastes people's time and energy, two of the most finite and precious resources we have in this world. Therefore, to waste someone's time, to *steal* someone's time, is also inhumane.

Words like *inhumane* may seem strong when talking about something like the business of Hollywood, but there are differing levels of inhumanity. The fact is that anything that treats people as a means to an end and not as an end in and of themselves is, to some degree or other, devaluing and dehumanizing to them. It is another form of abuse.

Because I felt so little love at home growing up, and because I had no love for myself, I'd found it in high school drama and in community theater. Those environments were genuinely supportive and rewarding. When you're a student, your education and development are the point of the whole endeavor. You are treated as the end and not merely as the means. In Hollywood, the opposite is true most of the time.

Being a professional actor is like being a door-to-door salesman, only instead of a vacuum cleaner, the product you're selling is yourself. Imagine going door-to-door and trying to convince every person you meet to like you, and 99 percent of the people say, "No, I don't like you." Now, put a rational, healthy person in that circumstance and they will understand that it isn't personal. The casting director who doesn't want to hire you isn't trying to hurt you as a person. They're just trying to make their movie, and you're not right for the role. But good luck trying to convince a twenty-one-year-old man-child with massive mommy issues that it isn't personal.

Do you have an empathetic heart? What inhumanities do you personally resonate with, and how do you process them?

Have you ever been treated as a means to an end? What happened and what have you learned from the situation?

DAY 27

Gold Stars

The real satisfaction I got from my work was when I'd get a call from my agent saying, "Hey, they're interested in you for this job." That would give me a big dopamine boost: *ping!* It meant that my hard work and my talent were being recognized. Then the call after that would be, "Hey, they want you for this job." Another dopamine boost: *ping!* Then the call after that would be, "Hey, look at this great deal that they're offering you, which means they value you and we are good to go." *Ping! Ping!* Then the call after would be, "Hey, we've heard from set that you're crushing it and everyone's happy with your performance." *Ping! Ping! Ping! Ping!*

I loved that shit. I fed off it, because it was love from the decision-makers and authority figures in the industry. In other words: from the parents. I was still subconsciously looking for love and approval and protection from grown-ups, the same love and approval and protection I never really got from my parents. Receiving that approval at all those steps along the way meant that I was accomplishing what I had set out to do. And if I wasn't getting those signals of approval, then that meant I was screwing up somehow. I was failing.

Even though on the surface it looks like you're thriving, the mommy and daddy issues and all of the trauma you haven't properly dealt with will always return. You'll always look for reassurance and recognition from others if you haven't worked through your issues. I was looking for a gold star from people who didn't give a shit about me and who would drop me at the first glimmer of a decline in ratings and viewership.

Do you look for gold stars from people who don't actually care about you? If you answered yes, why do you think that's the case?

Do you have trauma or parental issues that you haven't properly worked through? If you answered yes, what steps can you take to work through these issues?

An Endless Chase

There were many trials for the TV series *Chuck*. One was that the show was not a hit, but it was also not *not* a hit. We always did just okay, and that meant we were always on the bubble. I would have done anything to make *Chuck* work. I would have driven Toyota minivans from coast to coast if I'd been asked and if it would have actually helped. I was driven by my desire to bring joy to the fans who loved the show. I was driven by my love for my fellow cast and crew and my desire to protect them. But I was also being driven by my own insecurities, by my need to be perfect to avoid feeling like a failure, by my need for approval and acknowledgment from the decision-makers and my peers in the industry. Not only was I not getting it; I felt like I was getting the opposite of it.

In five years on *Chuck*, I gave every ounce of who I was to that show. I jumped through every hoop. On top of the eighty-hour weeks, I made every public appearance, tap-danced and schmoozed through every industry dinner, whatever I needed to do to help the show survive. They took every ounce that I gave them. But if I went back and asked for any kind of consideration in return—say a lighter shooting schedule, or a raise—the studio head told me flat out, "You know, you're lucky to have a job." He told me, in essence, that ultimately I wasn't worth very much to them, and because deep down I already believed I was worthless, it was a debilitating cycle in which to be stuck. It was terrible for my physical, emotional, and mental health. And because I didn't understand my true motivations—that I was looking for love and approval from people who would never give it to me to try to fill this bottomless well of need inside myself—I just kept doing it, even though it was slowly killing me.

Have you allowed your insecurities to drive you toward an endless chase of perfection and affirmation?

What can you do to prevent yourself from chasing the approval of others?

DAY 29

Armor

By any objective standard of "success," I have done well. During the time before I landed in Austin in 2017, anyone who looked at me would have seen a TV star with fame and money. But given the nature of my job, being beholden to parental surrogates and authority figures who could seemingly never be pleased, what looked to the whole world like a "successful" acting job was in fact pouring salt in the wounds I'd endured all through my childhood. I had invested my entire sense of self-worth in the Hollywood system that is not geared at all to care about my actual well-being as a person.

And yet: I never broke down. Never once in the five years that I filmed *Chuck* did I experience the kind of mental collapse that would come later in 2017. Starting from childhood, my ego had built up all these defense mechanisms to protect me from my mom's abuse, and my defenses held. All my tricks and tools and schemes of self-medicating and propping myself up, they kept me going. And therein lies the irony of what the ego does. It creates this armor to protect you from abuse, but the armor that protects you from abuse is the very thing that allows you to continue abusing yourself. You keep going and rationalizing your abusive reality more and more, wholly unconscious of the fact that your armor is taking a beating and that eventually, *inevitably*, it's going to crack.

Can you relate to the defense mechanisms that Zac's ego created to protect him? Have you created similar mechanisms to keep going and rationalize your reality?

Did your armor eventually crack? If so, how did you repair your armor?

Difficult

There was a point in 2017 when I was ready to break down. All of my traumas had started playing themselves out day after day. I was becoming, in the parlance of the industry, "difficult." I had lost faith in the entire system, and in turn I'd lost my faith in nearly everyone in it. There's a reason that actors, often more than those in other artistic disciplines, get pinned with being "difficult." It's because our names and faces are always the ones on the line. If a movie succeeds, we're probably given too much of the credit, but when a movie sucks, we're the first ones people blame. But filmmaking is an extremely collaborative medium. What you see on the screen is the result of the work of hundreds, sometimes thousands, of people, everyone from the set designers to the score composers.

And of all of those people, despite all the credit and blame we're assigned, actors by and large have very little power over the finished product. The writers, directors, and producers control most of what you say and do. The director and editor make all their cuts, and then the executives have the final say on what the movie will ultimately be. They have total control over what parts of your performance they want the public to see, and in the wrong hands that can be a career killer. An astute critic or viewer will watch a film and recognize what's the fault of the actor and what's not, but for the average moviegoer, the movie's success or failure is often inseparably attached to the faces that carry you through the story. As an actor, anytime you make a film or a TV show, you carry a disproportionate amount of the liability for the finished product, but you have practically zero agency or power or control over how that product is ultimately made, other than just showing up and playing your individual role as best you can. For a class of people who are prone to anxiety and problems of self-image to begin with, it's practically designed to engineer a mental breakdown. Add to that the modern pressure of social media, where everyone is judging you and giving you instant feedback on everything you do 24-7, and it's a wonder people can even function.

Can you relate to Zac's label of "difficult"? If you can,
why was that label unfair and what repercussions
did that label have on your self-worth?

DAY 31

Forgiveness

It's absolutely necessary to build healthy boundaries with people who've hurt and abused you in life, but boundaries are only one part of it. You can build walls to keep out everyone who's ever hurt you, but you'll still be dying alone inside your own castle if you're not doing the work, *your* work, to get healed.

Christians frame Jesus' teachings in philosophical and theological terms, but if you read His teachings a slightly different way, His message of forgiveness is a super intuitive understanding of human psychology that was way ahead of its time. Among the many concepts I think Jesus understood better and sooner than anyone else was forgiveness. We all want forgiveness for our sins and our faults. But the only way to forgive yourself is to accept that you were programmed that way, that you didn't have a choice in your parents or how you came up as a child, and that's not your fault. But guess what? In order to apply that logic to yourself, you now have to apply that logic to everyone else in the world. The only way to achieve forgiveness for our own sins is to learn how to forgive others for theirs—including our parents.

As has been said many times in many ways, refusing to forgive someone is like drinking poison and hoping that the other person will die. Forgiveness is not only, or even really, about the other person. Forgiveness is coming to the end of your ego and radically accepting that the pain caused by this person isn't personal. It's pain that they're passing on because it was passed on to them. It's generational trauma. It's unhealed hearts and minds damaging other hearts and minds. This is why it's so important to radically accept and radically love yourself and others at every turn. Finding the way to a place of forgiveness is difficult for everyone.

Think of someone you have forgiven. How did
you benefit from forgiving that person?

How do you think forgiveness, in your own
life, changes generational trauma?

DAY 32

It's Not Your Fault

There's a powerful scene in the movie *Good Will Hunting*, the emotional climax of the film, where Matt Damon's character, Will Hunting, and Robin Williams's therapist character both acknowledge the abuse they suffered from alcoholic fathers growing up. All through the film, Will has been putting up his tough-guy act, relying on a lifetime's worth of defense mechanisms to avoid reckoning with his terrible childhood and all the bad, self-destructive choices he's made in the years since, choices that have hurt the very people in his life who are trying to help him. Then, over the course of this one scene, his tough-guy act starts to fall apart as Robin Williams looks him in the eye and then hugs him and says to him, over and over again, "It's not your fault. It's not your fault. It's not your fault."

The reason we're so afraid to confront the problems of our past is because we're ashamed of them. We're ashamed of what we feel. We're ashamed of the bad choices we've made. We're ashamed because we believe those bad choices were our fault—that those mistakes and those feelings of worthlessness are who we are. But they're not. By and large, the trauma and the bad programming that led us to make those mistakes has less to do with us and has almost everything to do with the way we were raised. We look at the truly damaged people in society, the people who commit awful crimes or hurt other people in unimaginable ways, and we say that they're evil and there's no good in them, and our answer is always to punish them and shame them more, which simply has the opposite effect of stopping the madness. Instead of seeing the abused child in them and helping that child to heal, we dehumanize them, severing from them any amount of empathy or grace, and in turn amplify their propensity to abuse.

I don't believe those people are evil. They may commit evil acts, but they are humans. They're children of God. They're damaged. They need to be hugged tight and told, "It's not your fault. It's not your fault. It's not your fault." Of course, it's not that simple, which is one of the tricky things society has yet to figure out. It's said that if we admit that damaged people are not at fault for who they are, then we've absolved them, and the wrongs they've done are no longer their responsibility. But that's not the case. Both can be true at the same time: it may not be your fault, but it's still your responsibility. When it comes to the way we talk about these issues, we need to understand that explaining someone's behavior isn't the same as excusing it. If you have pain and bad programming and feelings of worthlessness inside you, that is not your fault. But when your pain has caused you to hurt other people, accepting and dealing with the consequences of your choices is still your responsibility.

Do you need to hear and acknowledge
that *it's not your fault*?

Are you struggling with understanding a loved one's
behavior? If so, how can you acknowledge their
behavior without damaging your self-worth?

DAY 33

Shields Built on Faith

One of the hardest parts of my relationship with my dad is our different approaches to faith. We share some elements in our beliefs, and I appreciate his faith, but I think he hides behind it. He'll sometimes use it as a shield, as an excuse. When my mom and dad finally got divorced, he didn't have it in him to fight her anymore. He was cooked. She'd chewed him up and spit him out so much that he didn't have it in him to co-parent with her or even fight her for custody. Then came the moves—ours to Seattle and his to Charlotte—and that pulled us permanently apart. But my dad has always used his faith to gloss over that rupture. He told me many times growing up that he agonized over it and prayed over it, but that he always came to the same conclusion.

"Son," he'd tell me, "I was so worried and I was praying and calling out to God, and the Lord said, *Darrell, don't worry. They're My kids. I've got 'em.* And I knew you kids were going to be fine."

For a long time, I used to think, *Wow, that's amazing. How cool that God told him that. And look at us, here we are. God did take care of us. We're alive. We're okay.*

Except we weren't okay by a long shot. Because what he did was leave us in the hands of someone who was emotionally and mentally unbalanced, and we suffered the consequences of that and are still suffering the consequences of that. Our dad could have been a shield, the first line of defense, but he wasn't.

My mom would always wield that fact as a weapon whenever she was angry at him. "Your dad didn't *fight* for you," she'd say. "Your dad didn't *want* you." As a kid I always defended him. "But you're the one who moved us to Seattle," I'd shoot back. "What was he supposed to do, keep following us around?" But now, as

I've gotten older and watched my sisters and friends have kids of their own, I've realized, "Well, yeah. That is what the fuck you're supposed to do. They're your kids. They're your responsibility." But in his brokenness and unhealed trauma, my dad had genuinely allowed himself to believe that God had absolved him of that responsibility.

Is there someone in your life who you believe hides behind their faith? If so, why do you think they're hiding?

How do you communicate with people who believe God has absolved them of their responsibilities?

DAY 34

Jesus-Level Forgiveness

Jesus' concept of forgiveness was wild in its time, and I don't think we fully grapple with that fact even to this day. We've glossed over it in such weird ways. We treat forgiveness like it's a traffic fine. The person says, "I'm sorry," and you say, "I forgive you," and that's that. But forgiveness is much deeper and more three-dimensional. Forgiveness is genuinely being done with something. Forgiveness is finding resolution and closure.

Ultimately, forgiveness is radical acceptance. It is radical love. It's understanding whatever someone did to you was because of their brokenness, not because of you and not because they are a "bad person." They had bad programming, and that led them to cheat on you, hit you, yell at you, whatever. "Forgive them, Lord, for they know not what they do." It's not a random platitude plucked from the Bible. It's a profound insight into the ways in which generational trauma shapes who we are and how we treat other people, even in ways we do not understand. If Jesus could ask God to forgive the Romans who crucified Him, who are we to deny that forgiveness to the trespasses others commit against us?

Do you agree that Jesus' concept of forgiveness was wild? Why or why not?

DAY 35

Real-Life Relationships

Love and relationships are complicated. They're even more complicated if you weren't loved as a child or if you experienced childhood trauma. Being with someone feels good, and so we assume this good feeling must be love, so we chase after it, and I did. I remember one of the first serious relationships I had, I jumped in headfirst and I gave that relationship everything I had. I was that guy showing up and surprising the girl with flowers and poems and all that hopeless-romantic kind of crap. It was all shit that I learned in the movies because where else are you supposed to learn how to proclaim your love for someone?

I was Lloyd Dobler from *Say Anything*, standing outside the girl's window with Peter Gabriel blasting on the boom box. Only this wasn't the movies. This was real life, and those stunts aren't necessarily romantic in real life. The movies create cinematic moments you want to re-create, but the reality is, no one really wants to be part of that type of story. Nobody wants the other person to give themselves over on day one. Nobody wants the other person to almost completely self-sacrifice right out of the gate—it's not attractive. We're not built to handle that other person's heart and that level of responsibility. It's overwhelming. But, when it comes to love, you don't learn what not to do until you've fucked up and did the thing you shouldn't do. It's really trial and error at its best.

Have you ever professed your feelings with a cinematic
gesture that ended up being a grand production?

Have you ever been the recipient of a
larger-than-life romantic gesture?

DAY 36

Callbacks Met with Disappointment

When I was depressed, one of the few developments that pulled
me out of my funk, at least temporarily, was getting a call from
James Gunn, who was directing the new *Guardians of the Galaxy*
film for Marvel. He wanted me to come in and audition for the
lead role of Star-Lord. I went in and auditioned. They liked me.
Then I got a callback. I got a screen test. This was the actual *lead*

in the next big Marvel franchise. I felt like I was *soooo* close. I even started to let myself think, *Oh my God, this might actually happen . . .*

But it didn't happen. Chris Pratt, who was everyone's first choice but who'd been saying he wasn't sure he wanted to do it, finally agreed to do it, and that was that. In the moment, it sucked, obviously, because I had wanted it so much, not fully realizing the reasons why I felt I *needed* it. The psychological ramifications were only beginning, and over the course of the next few years, losing out on that part really started to wreck me.

Chris is a great guy and is super talented, and he deserves every bit of success he's achieved, but for me, in that moment, it was soul crushing seeing his face plastered all over the world. His handsome mug was on every newsstand, every airport kiosk, one after another after another. It was this constant reminder: *You blew it, Zac. You're not good enough. You could have done it. It was so close, but you fucked it up. You just fucked it up.* Chris was off on this incredible trajectory, and I wasn't. At the time, it felt like one of those *Sliding Doors* moments, where you see how your whole life could have changed in an instant and gone a completely different and amazing direction. It was such a bitter pill to swallow.

Of course, that's how it felt at the time. In hindsight, I know that I wasn't ready for the responsibilities that would have come with that blessing. In the emotionally fragile state I was in, if I'd shot to the A-list like Chris did with *Guardians*, I might have crashed and burned in an even more grisly way than I eventually did. Looking back, I know God was telling me that I needed to prepare myself for His blessings before He could give them to me. But boy, it didn't feel that way at the time.

Have you ever thought you would receive a job offer or receive recognition but were met with disappointment?

Do you believe that everything happens for a reason when it comes to these situations? How has this proven true in your life?

DAY 37

Marriage

My marriage lasted less than a year. We lived in Toronto for a while and then moved back to LA. Every time we were in public we put up the facade that we were "great" and everything was "great," and isn't life "great"? Then we'd be alone and we'd be fighting and miserable. I didn't know what reality was anymore. We tried couples' therapy. Even agreeing to try it seemed like a huge leap forward, but it was too little, too late.

In early December we decided to separate. We spent all of Christmas and New Year's wrestling with whether we could still make things work, but it was pretty clear the end was inevitable. After the holidays, I flew off to Toronto to film a new show, and I'd barely been there a day when I got an email from her saying that she was filing for divorce. I wrote her back in tears, saying, "I'm sorry, I'm sorry, I'm sorry. I love you, and I hope you find somebody who loves you as much as I do, because I really, really do." And I did. And I do. I still love her as a person and want nothing but the best for her and her family. But loving her was never my problem. The problem was I didn't love myself, and so I put myself in a position where I had hurried into a relationship that wasn't healthy for either of us. If I had loved myself more, I could have loved her from afar as her friend. Unfortunately, I didn't know any better at the time.

I hated myself for putting myself in that type of relationship. I already struggled with loving myself. Some days I even struggled with liking myself. I judged myself harshly all the time. My self-talk was horrible. I generally took great pride in looking at all the variables and preparing myself ahead of time and not falling into traps and not being duped, so the reality of divorce was brutal.

Have you suffered through a loving experience because you didn't love yourself?

Have you hurried a relationship because you wanted desperately for it to work out? How did it turn out?

DAY 38

Acceptance

To this day my relationship with my dad isn't what I want it to be. He still maintains in his own heart that he didn't do anything wrong, that God is good and God had a plan, and look how it all turned out with my sisters married with nice families and me being this successful actor and it's all okay. Even if I wanted to get a better father out of him now, I don't think I could. Our relationship has always been pretty surface-level, and it remains that way. It's sad and it sucks and it hurts, but that's life. I know I can't change my dad and I can't fault him either, because I know what he's gone through in his life. I don't feel animosity toward him either. And I haven't made any ultimatums of "You either go and do this therapy or you're not in my life anymore." I see that scared little boy in him, afraid to confront the past, so I've learned not to press it.

I've learned that I can only control me. After working on myself I've developed a renewed vision for my relationship with my father. I will love him for exactly who he is. If our relationship never gets deeper, or stronger, that will be okay—and it is okay. Even if my relationship with my dad isn't what I wished it would be, I've grown to accept that it is the best relationship that it can be. My dad understands that I love him, and I understand that he loves me. Sometimes to live a full life, we have to accept relationships for what they are and stop trying to make them into something they never will be.

Do you have a relationship that you've tried to mold into something it's not? If you do, who is that relationship with, and have you accepted that you can't change it?

Have you ever given someone an ultimatum? If you have, did it work?

DAY 39

Love Is the Answer

If there is any point in this life, it is to love. I strongly believe that love is the answer to a lot of things that we're overthinking and overanalyzing. If you are acting as a conduit of light and love, if that is your only purpose in this world, then you are doing your job—and you are doing it efficiently and at the highest level if you've done it for yourself first.

Self-love is putting on your oxygen mask before helping anybody else. When you struggle with loving yourself, then you really struggle with allowing someone else to love you because you don't think you're deserving of it. You don't even know that you're doing that, but you are. So love yourself and go use what you have to be a conduit of love and light and life, and know that if you do, when you are finally extinguished and your time here is through, you will have done your part in this snap of a finger that is your lifespan on this miracle of a fucking planet.

Do you agree with Zac that the point of
life is to love? Why or why not?

How has self-love changed your life? Why are you
a better person when you love yourself first?

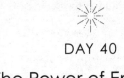

DAY 40

The Power of Empathy

Because I didn't love myself, over the course of my life, time and
again I've attracted a number of surrogate moms—older women
who've recognized me for who and where I was and tried in
various ways to protect me, love me, and encourage me. They
were essentially moms who weren't my mom, women who felt
compelled to stand in the gap for me and comfort me and pray
for me.

Unsurprisingly, I immediately fell into a similar pattern with my companion at the therapy facility in Connecticut. I showed up for breakfast one morning and she made me bacon and eggs, which is pretty much the most "mom" thing a person can do. As we got to know each other, not only did I learn that she was the wife of the pastor of the church I'd chosen to attend while I was out there; she also told me that she'd been given my first name a week and a half before I arrived, so she'd already been praying for me daily. It was such an incredibly meaningful gesture of kindness at a moment when I couldn't have felt more unlovable. This woman was incredibly empathetic with what I was struggling with. In fact, she was quite possibly the most empathetic person I'd ever met—the definition of the word. I could feel her feeling my pain, but she was able to do it in a way that never derailed her the way my empathy often derailed me.

Yes, it was her job, but she cared. You can always tell when you're dealing with someone who cares about their work versus someone who's just punching a clock. There's a marked difference, and Beth was definitely the former. She had a purity about her. I would almost say a childlike innocence, though not in a sense of naivete but of joie de vivre. And as pure and wholesome as she was, there was never a feeling that she had not lived life or evaded pain, loss, and doubt. She had done all of that yet remained this sunny, delightful presence in spite of it. With Beth, I felt right away that she got me, that she felt me. Often when you're struggling with something, you feel your pain is so unique that there's nobody you can talk to about it because nobody will understand it. I never felt that way with Beth. I never felt judged by her. I never felt a lack of understanding from her.

Have you received empathy from an individual who left a lasting impression on you?

Why do you think empathy is such a powerful gesture?

DAY 41

Deep Faith

I've always tended to see meaning where others see coincidence. I just have. I've always had a deep faith. I believe our lives intersect with specific people because we will have a deeper connection with those people, and meeting each other will provide a deeper understanding of our own lives. I also believe that there are certain times when people enter your life because it is part of God's plan.

When I was a kid, even as young as six or so, I understood faith. I could wrap my little head around the concept that there was a God and that God loved me. I'm never going to say that I know exactly who or what God is, because I don't think that any of us can or will ever understand that, but I've always felt the Creator's presence and love in my life.

I grew up in a very spiritual home, but because my father left us, it was not necessarily a very religious one. While my father's faith ran deep and the religious rituals gave his life the structure he took comfort in, my mother's faith—surprise, surprise—was the exact opposite. My mom took us to church almost zero times. Occasionally, if we were visiting friends in another place and they had a church that they liked, we might pop in, but it was rare. We did go to this church camp in the summertime, but that was a day care more than anything else. I'd say we probably went to Catholic Mass with Grandma Pat more than we ever went to church with my mom.

I don't think that you must go to church every Sunday to believe in God and know that He has a plan for you. I believe that deep faith is accepting His plan and allowing Him to take the reins.

Did you grow up in a religious home?

How has your faith changed as an adult?

DAY 42

You Are Loved

I think a lot of people go and get mental health treatment, and the reason their treatment doesn't ultimately hold is because they leave there learning a lot and knowing a lot but still feeling like a piece of shit. They don't have a person to hold them and say, "You're loved. You're worthy of love." That was certainly the case for me. And I completely understand that therapists and the staff at these facilities are legally not allowed to provide physical support in that sense.

But my deepest ailments—my inability to love myself, my inability to recognize my own self-worth—could only be fixed with love. I needed another human being to love me in order to show me the way to loving myself. The relentless prayer and empathy that Beth shared with me while I was at the Connecticut therapy facility is one of the major reasons I was saved.

Despite everything I had learned up to that point, my depression and pain and agony had persisted because of the one thing

I still did not understand: Knowing how to fix a machine is not enough. Ultimately, you have to believe that the machine *deserves* to be fixed. That you are worthy of the healing you seek.

DAY 43

Maintenance

Maintaining your mental health is a lifelong process. It's not a one-and-done. It's not "I got sick. I took antibiotics. Now it's gone and I don't have to worry about it anymore." Or, to compare it to caring for your teeth, if you don't brush and floss and stay vigilant, you're going to continue to have problems. Even if you go and get a root canal, if you don't start practicing proper care and maintenance of your teeth, you're just gonna keep needing more root canals.

I think part of the reason I was in denial about the never-ending aspect of coping with mental health was that, at the time of my breakdown, I felt like such a downer. It was depressing to think that I'd never put it behind me, that I would always be wrestling with these demons. I don't think that way anymore. Learning to deal with our trauma and learning how to love ourselves is simply the business of life. It is part of what it means to be a life-form on this little blue dot. It is neither good nor bad—it simply is.

More than that, however, seeing mental health as a never-ending struggle actually helps you. Once you see this as a journey with peaks and valleys, once you understand that the good times won't necessarily last forever, that gives you the perspective to finally understand that the bad times won't last forever either. There is always a dawn that follows the darkness.

Have you been guilty of not viewing
mental health as a lifelong process? If so,
what made you change your view?

How do you maintain your mental health?
What resources do you rely on?

DAY 44

The Power of Prayer

Even as my faith has evolved over the years, one thing I have
always held on to is the power of prayer and its ability to bring
peace. And if prayer has real power behind it, the people who
are willing to pray with and for you are the absolute proof of that
power. Faith the size of a mustard seed can move a mountain; I
think Jesus talked about ideas like that for a reason.

Ultimately, I'm not sure any of us, using all our facets and capabilities, can say who God is. But it's people who stand by you in prayer, those who genuinely believe in the power of prayer and whose faith is bigger than a mustard seed, who give us a glimpse of who God is. It is said that wherever two or more are gathered in God's name, God is there. I can attest to that because I have experienced it. Through prayer with other wonderful people, I have found the peace I was searching for. I will never be able to poetically explain the actual power of prayer, but I know it is something that you feel in your soul. Prayer can change your life.

Have you experienced the power of prayer? If so, what happened and who prayed with you?

DAY 45

A Perfect Storm

One thing about working, aside from the little dopamine hits of self-worth it gives you every day, is that you don't have a lot of downtime to sit around and beat yourself up. When Covid-19 struck, everyone suddenly had nothing but time to beat themselves up. A lot of people found a way to use the crisis to find and build a positive purpose. Some people banded together in a sense of community, bringing meals and medical supplies to isolated people in need. Others used the forced isolation and downtime to take on whatever projects they'd never been able to make time for, like painting the house or arranging all their digital photo albums.

A healthy person is capable of doing that. They get up every morning and say, "Oh my God, I have all this free time to invest in myself, I'll finally learn how to play guitar. I'll get to work and write that screenplay!" Then, once you do that, you've got the positive feedback loop going. Every day you've got a few more pages of screenplay or you've learned a new chord on the guitar, and you feel like you're accomplishing something. I couldn't do any of that. During the forced isolation I was back to hating myself, not loving myself enough to want to invest in myself at all. I was waking up in the mornings with major panic attacks. I was utterly depressed, crying, and shot through with anxiety and fear for myself and for the world.

The pandemic was a perfect storm. When the pandemic struck, I was in the middle of writing a book. Coincidentally the book was about my mental health journey and finally having it together; however, Covid-19 had me questioning whether I really had it together enough to write a book.

Eventually, I screwed up some courage, called my editor and my agent, and laid it out for them. "I still want to do it," I said, "but I can't do it right now. I don't know how to write a book about loving myself when I don't, currently, love myself." Fortunately, they were incredibly gracious, as I hoped that they would be. The world is full of people who accept you as less than perfect and understand why you're less than perfect. They agreed to put the book on pause and told me to go take as much time as I needed to put myself back together again.

So that's what I did.

Have you ever been in a situation where your honesty was met with grace? If so, what happened and how did grace impact you?

DAY 46

Compassion and Mercy

You may feel that no matter how hard you've tried, it's simply not enough. That somehow you have not, and will not, live up to whatever standards have been set to deem us worthy. You may feel that while others deserve these things, you do not. After having gone through my own darkness, and finding light on the other side, I can assure you that you are deserving of kindness. You are deserving of love and patience and forgiveness.

When you're struggling, it's hard to believe that other people are experiencing the same feelings of worthlessness and infe-riority. The road to better mental health is a long and difficult one. You will stumble and fall. You will slip up in a thousand little ways, daily. You will fall backward into old destructive patterns, again and again and again. And if you treat every one of those setbacks as a personal failure, you will never make it. The only way forward is to get back up, dust yourself off, and take another step. The only way to do that is to accept yourself as less than perfect. And the only way to do that is to have compassion and mercy for yourself.

We give grace and extend compassion to others relatively easily. Why do you think we tend to be harder on ourselves than other people?

What are three ways you can grant compassion and mercy to yourself right now?

DAY 47

Addicted

When I look back, what I see clearly is that all my life I've been addicted to something, anything, to bring me happiness. Whether it was video games, rollerblading, or entertaining people, I was probably addicted to it. I discovered those diversions and I binged on them the same way other people do with drugs and gambling and food. I always needed to go and find and do more to make myself happy, to get away from the chaos of my homelife and my abusive parents and being bullied at school. I had no idea that the whole time I was bingeing on those things, what I was really doing was jamming down as hard as I could on the levers in my brain to create as much dopamine as possible to make me happy. I was making myself a glutton for joy and pleasure and happiness in order to avoid pain.

But there's a serious downside to that. Among the scientists who study dopamine and its effects, one consensus is that the pleasure created by dopamine is controlled by a lever in our minds: the pain/pleasure lever. Pain and pleasure, it turns out, are deeply correlated with each other. Our brains light up in almost the exact same way when we experience either of them. Back in the hunter-gatherer days, there wasn't so much going on in the way of "fun." You were hunting, you were gathering, you were making camp, you were building a fire. You were tracking a bear for twenty miles and then killing it with your tribesmen. These things sucked. Maybe there was a little time at the end of the day to sit in a circle and tell some stories or go off and have sex, but that's about it. A lot of life for our ancestors was pain and endurance, and what researchers have found is that when you press down hard on the pain side of the lever, once you let up on that, your body steps in to counterbalance the lever. It rewards you with a rush of dopamine to bring your body back into equilibrium, and man, it feels good. It's why some people get addicted to ultramarathons and going to the gym, because the rewards are so intense.

But the flip side is true as well. When you overdose on pleasure, you have to pay the piper on the other side. In trying to self-medicate my trauma, I was overdosing in pleasure. Whether it was hearing the roar of the crowd or a weekend-long party with friends, I was trying so hard to feel good. Then, when these

106

perfect storms would come along, like a relationship ending or being out of work, I would lose my ability to keep pressing on the pleasure side of the lever and it would flip hard the other way, causing me to plunge far deeper into the darkness than any healthy, well-balanced person would. That is the downward spiral of dopamine deficiency.

Have you made yourself a glutton for joy and happiness so you could avoid pain?

What are some ways you can regulate your pleasure in your life?

Losing Someone You Love

It's sad when people don't think that they're loved, and it takes them dying for everyone to be able to come back together and celebrate them. Knowing how much pain my mother suffered in life, and knowing that she wasn't in pain anymore, allowed me to tell myself that her death wasn't a tragedy. In that sense, I could see it as a kind of gift, and I held on to that thought as a kind of silver lining. But there was no escaping the overwhelming sadness we all felt, because it *was* tragic.

It was tragic that such a beautiful, talented, intelligent, charming, dynamic, and vibrant woman ended up destroying herself without ever being able to live the life she could have lived. It was tragic that she died without ever having the opportunity to reconcile with her parents, her siblings, her ex-husbands, or her children. When you know that somebody is going to die, even someone you've had major issues with, you still want to be able to let them know that you do love them before they're gone, and the fact that we didn't get that chance with my mother is one of the saddest and hardest things about losing her the way we did.

Losing my mother forced me to recognize how precious life is and how equally precious the people in your life are. Don't take for granted the time you have with your loved ones.

Have you lost someone without being able
to truly convey how you felt about them?

Is there someone in your life that you love but it's a
complicated situation? How can you let them know that
you care about them without getting into an argument?

Considering Medication

The decision to take or not take medication had been an issue that exacerbated the problem. If there is always a correct choice, is the correct choice for me to take the medication or not take the medication? Of course, as I now understand, there is no correct choice. Not for that. You go and you try to do things in earnest because you're trying to care for yourself. Maybe it works, maybe it doesn't, but in making that attempt, you're hopefully finding more tools for your tool belt along the way.

I want to be clear. I'm not saying, "Take medication and it will solve your mental health problems." Medication might help you, or it might not. The importance of the medication for me, beyond its actual physiological effects, was the pivotal, seminal turning point it symbolized in my journey. When I left the therapy facility in Connecticut, I'd had a genuine breakthrough, believing that I finally was able to love myself enough to want to heal myself. Accepting that I might need medication, that I might need that stool to stand on to escape the darkness, was the moment I was finally able to say that I can still love myself even if I'm never able to fix myself. It was the moment I was finally able to stop beating myself up for failing to be this perfect version of who I thought I was supposed to be. It was the moment I finally learned to have grace with myself. True grace. God's grace.

What is your opinion on medication
for mental health issues?

When was the moment you finally learned
how to have true grace with yourself?

DAY 50

Fixing vs. Healing

I've amassed so many important tools during my mental health journey—meditation, prayer, the Enneagram, different therapeutic practices, better eating, better exercise—but simply having access to those tools would be meaningless without loving myself enough to use them and having grace with myself, forgiving myself, every time I fall short of where I want to be, which will inevitably happen. That's life. For the longest time I was obsessed with "fixing" my brokenness, when what I needed to do was *heal* it. As it turns out, there's a huge difference between the two. Fixing is a solution, a task with an endpoint. You follow steps one through four and then you're done and you mark it off your checklist. You're coming at yourself from a technical, analytical standpoint. "What's the problem? Let's get at the problem. Let's solve this. Let's do this." And you think that you're loving yourself because you're trying to help yourself, when the reality is you're not being patient or kind to yourself because all you're doing is judging yourself on whether you're fixing the problem or not.

Healing, on the other hand, is a process. It's an ongoing process, and it's never done. From a motivational or an attitudinal standpoint, you come at yourself a lot differently if you're trying to heal than if you're wanting to fix. To the extent that you are applying more grace and more empathy and more love to yourself as you are navigating behavioral patterns in your life, you are healing more than fixing. Healing is acceptance. It's being patient with yourself and not beating yourself up over unmet expectations, either yours or other people's, and not basing your worth on external validation.

Do you agree with Zac's depiction of the difference between fixing and healing? Why or why not?

What mental health resources have you recently used to heal?

DAY 51

Patience and Forgiveness

I never learned to have patience or forgiveness with myself, because I had parents who struggled to have patience and forgiveness with me, with each other, and even with themselves. The only way I learned how to treat myself was to be condescending, impatient, harsh, and critical. That was the only way I knew how to talk to myself. And that's not what good parenting is. Good parents help their children to tackle behavioral issues by being patient and telling the child that there is no shame or condemnation in what they've done, and that they love them regardless. All of these things seem obvious, but they aren't to so many parents. Or, more likely, parents think they're doing them correctly, but they're not.

We always want to tell abusive people, "Don't treat people like that. You should know better. You're a bad person." But everyone out there, and I mean *everyone*, believes that they're the good guy, the hero of their own story. My mom thought she should have been awarded "Mom of the Year." I have no doubt that in all of her yelling and screaming, she thought she was doing the right thing to fix whatever was "wrong" with her rowdy, rambunctious kids. She didn't know how to sit with us and our issues, because our issues were a reflection of her issues, and that was too much for her to handle.

My mother didn't love herself, nor could she forgive herself. Because it's hard. To this day, those old habits and that bad programming are still there, and I start to slip. I have to remind myself to give myself love and grace. It's a daily practice. But I do it because I know that practicing love and acceptance is the difference between breaking the cycle of generational trauma or continuing it. It is all that stands between the fate I've avoided and the fate to which my mother succumbed.

Did your parents endure trauma? What about your parents' parents?

What daily practices can you implement so you can grant yourself patience and forgiveness?

Trace Trauma and Discover Healing

I think it's important for people to talk about mental illness because it's one of the key ingredients to getting to the root of what's occurring. Silence is one of the major contributing factors to people feeling inescapably stuck in their depression, their anxiety, their stress, their fear, their shame. If you're suffering in silence, you're not going to find a solution for it, because nobody knows you're suffering. And we are not capable of getting ourselves out of a lot of these issues that we are facing, mentally and emotionally—particularly in today's society—by ourselves. We need help. We need each other. We need community. We need a tribe. We need family.

I'm convinced that all of the issues that we suffer from in this world are rooted in the broken heads and hearts of individuals. If we could go trace all of that down and heal it, we'd be taking care of the planet, we'd be taking care of the animals on the planet, and we'd be taking care of each other and ourselves.

We'd be doing that because we would not be acting out of our unhealed traumas or allowing ourselves to be led around by our broken egos in a constant state of fearing and fighting, which is ultimately where all our issues lie. But if we can all acknowledge these traumas and seek to heal and free ourselves from them, then perhaps we can start to truly listen to each other, learn from each other, and love each other.

Take time today to trace the brokenness in your family. Where do the issues lie? Acknowledge these traumas so you can seek out proper healing.

DAY 53

Manifest Positivity

All of that drama you see played out for public consumption in the tabloids—actors being difficult to work with or having temper tantrums or being divas—those are all manifestations of poor mental health. That person is scared inside. That person is being ripped apart by anxiety and fear. If Hollywood helps them to be less scared, they would make better movies and everyone will be happier and wiser, not to mention wealthier, because the team would have made a better movie. But that's not how Hollywood normally operates. It *normally* just milks people for as long as it can and then casts them aside when they're deemed no longer milky enough.

This way of life has filtered into our society. People are far more consumed with other people's opinions than they are with their own. There's a quote that says, "Other people's opinions are none of your business." Whoever said that couldn't be more right. It is important not to allow drama to take over your life and well-being. Shut down the background noise from other people and the unfiltered recommendations society inserts so you can manifest positive mental health.

What opinions should you dismiss from your life?

What steps can you take right now to manifest more positive mental health in your life?

DAY 54

The Cycle of Shame and Humiliation

I've seen firsthand with my parents how shame can take over an individual's life. When this happens, the person's psyche can't handle it. For example, with my dad, all of the trauma that he endured rendered him incapable of truly standing up and fighting for his own children. He was afraid to reckon with that because he was afraid it would bring on more shame. Because that's how we wrongly deal with so many things in our society.

When people admit wrongdoing, when they admit they have fallen short, they're rarely forgiven. Too often they're shamed and humiliated. Even though I was left hurting from parental neglect, I never wanted to shame and humiliate my parents. Just the opposite. I wanted them to experience the healing that lay on the other side of acknowledgment. However, with generational trauma and abuse, you can't expect people to heal since they are forced to live with the shame. Their shame creates more shame and more shame—you get the picture.

Does the cycle of shame and humiliation exist in your family?

What can you do to change your inner circle's view of shame and humiliation?

Happiness Held Hostage

I will never forget what my therapist said to me when I was discussing my frustrations with the relationship my father and I have. I was hell-bent on giving him an ultimatum. Either he goes to therapy to work on our issues or no contact. Looking back, I see that I was romanticizing the relationship into something it wasn't ever going to be. The reality was, I needed to accept the relationship for what it was.

My therapist said, "Your own happiness is still being held hostage by your father, by his being willing or unwilling to go and do this work that you think he needs to go do. If you're waiting for your father to go and do this, then your happiness is going to hinge on something that may or may not ever happen, so you're potentially never going to be happy—and you might end up losing your father in the bargain."

Ultimatums are created from insecurities and are a form of manipulation. It provides the illusion of choice, but there really isn't one. I was basically putting people on a hook unless they fit into the box I wanted them to be in. I was trying to force change because of my own OCD issues—which isn't fair. It is possible to have healthy boundaries and not force people to change.

What is your opinion of ultimatums? Has your opinion changed over the years? Why or why not?

Narcissism

It might take you by surprise or you might flat out be in denial, but did you know that nearly everyone shows traits of narcissism from time to time? Think about it. Have you ever exaggerated your importance? Have you ever been envious of someone? Have you ever been a little selfish and wanted the attention to be only on you? The difference between showing traits of narcissism and being an actual narcissist is that someone who only has traits takes accountability, has insight, and recognizes the narcissistic traits as wrong. A narcissist takes no accountability and allows the traits to become their personality.

I believe that my mother tried to love me, and very much did love me, with the understanding and tools available to her at any given time. But she never learned to fully love properly because she was never fully loved properly, and because of that, she never learned how to fully and properly love herself. That lack of self-love is what I think spawned her narcissistic tendencies. We tend to throw around the word *narcissist* a lot nowadays, so I don't use this term lightly. After doing the work I've done for my own well-being, I realize that we all struggle with bouts of narcissism. The things to ask yourself are just how deep the struggle is and how negatively is it affecting your life and the lives around you. For my mom, her inability to love herself left a massive hole that she didn't know how to fill without making things about herself. Her narcissism was her ego trying to keep her alive.

Think about the last time you displayed narcissist traits. What happened and how did you react? What did you learn from the situation?

Do you know someone who is a narcissist? How do you interact with them? What boundaries have you established?

DAY 57

A Third Party

Therapy is something that I think everyone can benefit from. One of the primary values of therapy, that the counselor is a disinterested third party, is also one of its primary drawbacks. Many of my sessions have felt impersonal and clinical. I'd be sitting in these therapists' offices, curled up in a ball in my chair, bawling my eyes out, snot and tears running all over the place, and the most they would do would be to gesture to where I could get myself a tissue when what I needed was a fucking hug.

I needed someone to grab me and swaddle me and hold me through my shaking and my crying and tell me it was going to be okay. But therapists don't do that. They can't do that. Which I totally get. I understand the need for a clinician to maintain a professional distance and not get emotionally involved with patients. It's for your benefit and theirs. I share this opinion because I would enter therapy thinking it would be a magical session and that I would walk out with some Ghandhi-like higher understanding. But until you actually learn to love yourself, you're not going to experience true progress. Your third party can't fix you but they can listen and guide you to better understand who you are and your purpose.

Do you think the vast majority of people have developed their opinions of how therapy works based on TV shows and movies?

Why do you think it is important for a therapist to be a disinterested party?

Keep Going

It's not a sprint; it's a marathon. I repeat this phrase to myself often because I need a reminder. And I think you do too. In a world where we can upload pictures and videos within seconds, where we can reach our loved ones via text or call instantly, and where everything is so rushed, I remind myself often that I'm just sprinting.

Sprinters are in for a short distance and marathon runners are long-distance. I've realized that both are essential to a balanced life because I don't actually know what is going to happen next. I've accepted that these are God's plans and not my own. Planning for the future sets me up for potential failure because apprehension and fear kick in when things change and feel unstable. I believe that mental wellness is a lifelong commitment, a marathon of sorts, but the resources and routine will evolve as you evolve. A marathon runner might keep running the same path, while a sprinter is agile and willing to switch things up.

While I want to remind myself mental health is a lifelong, marathon-like commitment, I understand the sprinter mentality encourages me to be amendable and not freak out when things make me feel uncomfortable and throw me off my regular path.

Do you agree with Zac's sprinter mentality? Why or why not?

How do you handle stress and struggles when you're forced to change your plans or routine?

DAY 59

A Greater Purpose

My agent emailed me about *Shazam!* while I was at the therapy facility in Connecticut. To be fair, the agency wasn't privy to the details. I thought the email was twisted but funny because I had *barely* reached a point where I was in a good state of mind—and they wanted me to play a superhero.

Then I remembered that God is always using us for a greater purpose, for other people's lives and the benefit of the world. We don't get to dictate how that goes, and maybe this opportunity was God reminding me that we always have to give our best to whatever is right in front of us.

Think about an experience when the timing didn't align but God was using you for a greater purpose.

DAY 60

The Perfect Role

I'd always dreamed of playing a role like Tom Hanks's in *Big*—
being a kid who magically becomes a grown-up—and *Shazam!*
was that same story only with superpowers, which was such a
fun idea to play with. On top of that, the story of *Shazam!* has
a biblical connection as well—albeit a subtle, yet still profound,
connection. It's a story set in a world of gods and demigods,
and the main enemy is the Seven Deadly Sins. I'd be playing a
superhero whose name is an acronym that starts with *S*—*S* for
Solomon, the wisdom of Solomon. Movies about mutants and

radioactive spiders are cool, but this was about a godly/godlike man fighting literal sin incarnate. I mean, c'mon!

Then there was Billy Batson himself: an orphan, abandoned and rejected by his mother. I wasn't an actual orphan, but I might as well have been in some ways. I kind of had parents growing up, but I kind of didn't, especially after I was twenty-one. I saw so much of myself in this character, this kid who wants to find acceptance and family. I suppose you can find correlations in anything if you look hard enough, but I felt so connected to the story and the character that I had to believe it was more than mere coincidence.

My role in *Shazam!* was God's timing and will. I was able to use the opportunity to talk about my mental health journey. It was an incredible way to destigmatize mental health issues. This was a full-circle moment for me and my mental wellness journey.

What personal struggles have made you stronger?

Why are challenges an integral part of being healthy?

About the Author

Zachary Levi has proven himself a triple threat—he is an accomplished actor, singer, and dancer—all of which were displayed in his Tony-nominated performance for "Best Leading Actor in a Musical" in the critically praised Broadway production *She Loves Me*.

Zachary will star in *Harold & the Purple Crayon* for Sony, based on the wildly popular children's book by Crockett Johnson. The film is slated for an August 2024 release in theaters. He recently wrapped production on Joe Carnahan's real-life survivor thriller *Not Without Hope* and is also set to star in *Hotel Tehran*, a new action thriller from writer-director Guy Moshe.

In March 2023, Levi reprised his role as Shazam! in the Warner Bros. DC franchise, *Shazam! Fury of the Gods*. Directed by David F. Sandberg, this film was the follow-up to the first installment, *Shazam!*, which held the #1 spot at the box office for weeks following its April 2019 release.

In 2021, Zachary portrayed iconic NFL MVP and Hall

of Fame quarterback Kurt Warner in *American Underdog* for Lionsgate, directed by Andrew and Jon Erwin. Zac will return with the Erwin brothers for another Lionsgate film *The Unbreakable Boy*, based on the true story of the most inspiring boy who touched and changed the lives of those around him.

In a fan-favorite recurring role, Levi took home a Screen Actors Guild Award for "Best Ensemble in a Comedy Series" for seasons two and three of Amazon Studios' Emmy-winning series *The Marvelous Mrs. Maisel*. The first season of the show won six Primetime Emmys, two Golden Globes, as well as a Peabody Award and two Critics' Choice Awards. The second season won one Golden Globe, three SAG Awards, one PGA Award, two Broadcast Film Critics Association Awards, one Critics Choice TV Award, and TV Program of the Year at the AFI Awards.

Previous film credits also include *Chicken Run: Dawn of the Nugget*; *Teddy's Christmas*; *Apollo 10½: A Space Age Childhood*; *Thor: The Dark World*; *Alvin & the Chipmunks: The Squeakquel*; and *Tangled*. The song "I See the Light," written for *Tangled* and performed by Levi and Mandy Moore, was nominated for an Oscar and Golden Globe for "Best Original Song." The pair performed the duet at the 83rd Annual Academy Awards ceremony. "I See the

Light" also won the Grammy Award for "Best Song Written for Visual Media" at the 54th Grammy Awards.

Levi is best known for another fan-favorite performance as Chuck Bartowski in the hit NBC series *Chuck*. Other TV credits include the miniseries *Alias Grace* and *Heroes Reborn*.

In June 2022, Levi made his authorial debut with his memoir *Radical Love: Learning to Accept Yourself and Others*, which shares his emotional journey through a lifetime of crippling anxiety and depression to find joy, gratitude, and ultimate purpose.

Levi currently serves as an ambassador to Active Minds, a nonprofit organization dedicated to raising mental health awareness among college students via peer-to-peer dialogue and interaction.

From the Publisher

GREAT BOOKS

ARE EVEN BETTER WHEN THEY'RE SHARED!

Help other readers find this one:

- Post a review at your favorite online bookseller

- Post a picture on a social media account and share why you enjoyed it

- Send a note to a friend who would also love it—or better yet, give them a copy

Thanks for reading!